THE PRODIGAL SON

A POETIC JOURNEY

Collin Lee

The Prodigal Son: A Poetic Journey
© 2025 by Collin Lee

ISBN: 978-1-958723-58-6.

This poetic journey is based on the Parable of the Prodigal Son found in the Gospel of Luke, Chapter 15.

Cover design by Toney Mulhollan and interior layout by Collin Lee.

About the author: **Collin Lee** is a graduate of the University of Southern California who has served in the full-time ministry in Los Angeles before starting a marketing career that spans more than 25 years. He also served as the first elder of his local congregation in Santa Clarita, California, where he continues to preach and teach alongside the church leadership. He is an experienced copywriter and an author of a National Gold IPPY Award-winning picture book, *The Efil Brothers.*

Theatron Press is an imprint of Illumination Publishers International www.ipibooks.com

To my dearest wife Sunny,
my Home Sweet Home

PREFACE

The parable of the Prodigal Son in the Gospel of Luke is considered the epitome of all Jesus' parables because of its detailed narrative and complex themes within: Love, forgiveness, repentance, redemption and even envy. It is one parable that clearly depicts the works of God in our lives.

And this is especially true for me.

Back in 1990, while I was studying aerospace engineering at the University of Southern California, I attended a Bible study. It was a small group of faithful students gathered at a campus apartment, and they were studying: The parable of the Prodigal Son in Luke 15. Although Christianity has been a part of my whole life, I was then an agnostic, and something profound happened. There was this certain desire within, and at the end of the Bible study, I went up to the student leader and said, "I'm coming home." As corny as it sounded, it was the beginning of my journey of becoming a born-again disciple of Jesus, for the first time.

And now, more than three decades later, I can look back and reflect on the ups and downs of my Christian life, and I am utterly grateful for what God has done.

Hence is this humble literary endeavor, a "letter of gratitude" per se to God and all those who guided me to remain faithful. It is a familiar story retold as a poetic journey, my attempt to bring the story of the Prodigal Son to life in my own small way.

My hope is that these words will remind you of God's love, patience and forgiveness.

Good reading.

In Him,
Collin Lee

The Younger Son

The green field stretched out to the horizon,

Too mundane,

The vastness of the blue sky above,

Too empty.

Each sunrise reeling in the glowing sunset,

The balmy breeze stroking over the harvest-

ready field,

The peaceful lowing of cows and bleating of

goats,

So beautiful,

They say,

But it is all the same.

Why am I here?

My youth screams,

The burning and yearning within,

It has to be more than this,

My passion for life explodes in my heart.

No,

No,

No,

This life of mine,

Jailed in this farmland,

Robs me,

Drowns me,

Kills me.

There is a whole world beyond that horizon,

I hear,

And it beckons,

My young heart to pound and thrust.

The excitement of the unknown,

Yet familiar,

Through those words of my friends who

have tasted the thrills,

So beautiful,

They say,

And my youth longs.

When will I embark?

When can I experience?

I must,

I must.

My youth is worth more than gold,

I must,

I must.

Before it is too late,

I must,

I must.

With my share of my father's estate,

I can,

I will.

Tomorrow is too late,

To have my share of the inheritance.

Today is the day,

I will.

There is no shame in that,

For it is mine to have,

Before it is too late,

I will.

The Father

Oh, time,

The inevitable,

The destined,

The river through life,

Taught me well,

To submit and surrender,

To the Heavenly One who created it all,

Over all,

And in all.

His greatest blessings,

I can count them,

Two that are,

My beloved sons,

My legacy when I am done.

The older is how older is,

Respectful and diligent,

The younger is how younger is,

Passionate and carefree.

The older one,

Reserved,

The younger one,

Restless,

Both are beloved.

Precious memories abound,

Both in their own ways,

Making my old days content and grateful.

From their births till now,

I witnessed the Heavenly One's shaping

hands on them,

Molding and allowing them to be who they

are now.

My old eyes smile,

Even when they fall,

Knowing those wounds would become

scars,

Apparent yet impervious,

Painful yet precious,

Lessons learned.

Their young souls still have much to learn,

Since wisdom draws from cries and tears.

The older one works the field,

Just as I have for all my life,

Just as my father had for all his life.

The younger one,

He works the field alongside his brother,

But I wonder,

His eyes are always on that distant horizon,

As if he could see for miles and beyond.

I wonder.

The Younger Son

My father,

Please do not refuse my request.

The younger that I am,

I am less than my brother.

Yet the life I desire,

Is so much more.

My father,

Please do not refuse my request.

The birthright of the firstborn,

The double portion of inheritance,

That I will never have.

Hence be gracious to me,

The second born,

Whom you hold dear,

And consider my youth,

The fire within,

That cannot be quenched.

All I ask,

Is just my portion of inheritance,

That I may have now,

For now is what I live for.

As far as the eyes can see,

The field and all that are in it,

Are for my brother,

And I do not envy.

But beyond what the eyes can see,

Is what I long for,

The unknown,

The possibilities,

The future.

Please let me,

Be someone other than,

A shadow of my brother.

Please let me,

Discover myself,

Not within the fence of your care,

But on my own,

Out there,

In the world,

Where anything is possible.

My father,

Please do not refuse my request.

The Father

My child,

The younger that you are,

But less than your brother,

That you are not.

You have all my heart,

As does your brother.

What you ask,

Is shunned by others,

But you are my child,

And I know your heart,

Young and restless,

As I was when I was,

My father's child.

What you ask,

Is not right in others' eyes,

But you are my child,

Whether you are right,

Or wrong.

Oh, I so wish you would stay,

Stay within my arms,

My child.

Yet I know,

Nothing will quench your heart's desire,

But only living it.

The world,

I have seen,

The world,

I have lived,

Full of grief and sorrow,

With temporary happiness,

Like the mist in the morning,

Fading ever too fast,

Days seem short,

Nights seem too long,

Dark and cold,

Even in the heat of summer,

The world,

That I know.

The aches in my heart,

I cannot deny,

Yet you will go anyway,

Whether with my blessing,

Or without.

So I will grant your request,

For my love for you,

Is deeper than you would ever know.

Heed my words,

My son,

Your eyes will see many things,

Your heart will feel many things,

The only thing I want you to remember,

If you hear that voice within,

Perhaps a whisper,

Or a loud cry,

Homeward bound,

Do not quell it,

But let it sink in,

Let it lead you,

Home.

The Teacher

Giving,

The father knew how,

Even when it tore him inside,

As if a part of him died.

A father's command,

Stay,

He could give,

But he knew well,

Obedience without willingness,

Is but an illusion.

All the years in the field,

Had taught him,

Labor and toil were his part,

But the harvest was not,

That of the domain,

Of the grace,

Of the Heavenly One.

Such is parenting,

Labor and toil were a parent's part,

But the future of a child was not,

Still the domain,

Of the grace and mercy,

Of the Heavenly One.

So the father bid his younger son farewell,

And watched him go,

Not knowing when,

Or even if,

His son would come back.

It was a beautiful day,

But in his heart,

It was raining,

Drenching the very soul of his,

With worries and sorrow.

The younger son, however,

Could only see what was ahead,

Finally,

The world that he only heard of,

Dreamed of,

Now would see with his own eyes.

His journey to the City,

Hasten he could,

With comfort,

As his inheritance turned into,

Money that everyone wanted.

Innkeepers welcomed him,

Carriages were luxurious,

Delicacies awaited him.

A wealthy young man,

Whose money,

His only possession,

Became something more,

His identity.

A stranger though he was,

People loved,

Who he was,

So he thought,

Too young to see,

The depths of people's hearts,

Dark and treacherous.

The Older Son

Oh, my brother,

Disrespectful,

Prideful,

Selfish,

Utterly sinful,

Has brought disgrace to our family.

His restless soul,

So loud even in the open field,

I knew,

One day he would,

Betray the love of the family.

May the Heavenly One guide him,

Through his follies,

Yet punish him,

To see the light.

This field that he was born into,

Is his destiny,

Not the City beyond the horizon.

Laboring and toiling under the sun,

Is his destiny,

Not carousing through the night.

May he return,

With a hard lesson learned,

That his life is not his own,

But a part of the family,

That our father's patience,

Is not a virtue to be exploited,

By his flippant heart.

Oh, my dear father,

Why so gracious and merciful,

When he is not worthy?

Why did you grant his request of defiance?

Where was the father's command,

So uncompromising and solemn?

Oh, I wish I was there,

When he asked for his inheritance,

For it would have been,

A scene of a godly judgment,

Righteous anger,

He would have witnessed.

Now that he is gone,

I must work,

Harder and longer.

Utterly unfair,

Indeed it is,

Yet my duty calls,

The firstborn,

The pride of the family.

The Father

Each day seems longer and longer,

When will my son return?

With the sunrise,

I gaze at the distant horizon,

Perhaps today?

As the sun hands over the day,

I look once again toward the wide open
field,

Perhaps tomorrow?

Has he arrived in the City safely?

Shall I send one of my servants?

I could,

But I shouldn't,

It is his life to live,

But it is the life I brought forth,

The wrestling within,

I can hardly bear.

Yet again,

The truth is,

Our lives are not in our hands,

But only within the palm of the Heavenly

One,

Who created and directs all things,

Sovereign and eternal.

So again,

I surrender all that I feel,

Knowing my son's wheel of destiny,

Continues to turn,

On it own course,

As is mine,

Mysterious and unpredictable,

No one can take the helm.

Hence we all,

Let.

The Younger Son

Oh, what a city!

It has everything to offer,

All my heart's desire,

Fulfilled.

Its beauty,

Marvelous,

Its grandeur,

Majestic,

Its culture,

Exotic,

Its power,

Undeniable.

It is the greatest,

That my eyes have ever seen.

People from all over the world,

Gathered to live together,

In harmony.

This is my new home,

My destiny.

And yes, friends,

So many,

So quickly,

How I enjoy their company,

As they do.

The long nights that my father worried,

Are not long at all,

Filled with drinks and laughter,

Only fade with the dawn.

Oh, this life of mine,

In this great City,

Is the ultimate,

For a young soul like mine.

Eat,

Drink,

Be merry,

A life as it is supposed to be,

Picture book perfect,

Envy of many,

Lucky,

They say,

But I know better,

It is mine,

Because I can.

The Teacher

The City has her many faces,

Her beauty,

Luring and trapping,

Those young souls from all over the world,

But her hidden side,

Only seen by the desperate,

Enslaving those youthful desires,

Deeper and darker,

Until no hope could be found.

Pleasure, pleasure,

A voice dripping with honey,

Yet more bitter than gall,

The taste at the end.

Wisdom, wisdom,

A lamp showing the way,

Yet a young soul cannot see,

The blindness of vanity.

The younger son,

Will in time find out,

Everything comes to an end,

As the dawn vanquishes the night.

Drinks will dry out,

Laughter will fade,

Friends will move on,

Only left with oneself.

His money,

His only possession,

Will come to naught,

Without notice.

What will he do then?

And now with famine approaching,

Things will go,

From bad to worse,

For a foreigner like him,

The City will feel,

Even more desolate,

Alone indeed,

Lost indeed,

No sense of direction,

Whether within or without.

The whirlwind of change,

Too tough to withstand,

Even for a youth,

With all his vigor.

What will he do then?

The Heavenly One will guide,

But never dictate,

The way one should go.

For in this freedom,

One understands,

Fate is a dance,

Between the Creator and the creation,

In harmony,

Comes a content life,

In discord,

Comes regrets.

So what will he do?

Sometimes the choices one makes,

Lead to no choice.

The Younger Son

Days have fled,

They went by too fast,

Those glorious nights,

Disappeared without a trace.

My friends,

Where are they now?

Those laughter and praises,

Raising of cups in my name,

Overflowing of silky wine,

Now only in my vague memory.

What I have now,

Is only myself,

No more money,

No more identity,

No one knows my name,

Anymore.

With famine at hand,

The City no longer shines.

With famine within,

Where can I go to rest my head?

Where can I taste a cup of water?

Where can I find food to eat?

The City that I love,

So I thought,

The City without,

It became.

As if a bolt from the blue,

My life has,

Turned for the worst,

Too fast for me to notice.

Indeed,

The days are too short,

The nights are too long.

How strange,

The coldness I feel,

Is not from without,

But from within.

The shivering,

Is of my soul,

Not of my body.

Yet I still try to cling,

To the voice of this City,

Possibilities, possibilities,

Bad will pass soon enough,

You can be anything you dream of.

As the night slowly blankets the City,

I must find,

A place to stay,

And perhaps,

A piece of myself.

The Teacher

Alas, in the midst of the storm of life,

Having lost his bearing,

Tossed by loneliness,

Hunger,

Hopelessness,

The younger son wandered,

Around the City,

He so loved,

So he thought.

Each night,

Brought fear and uncertainty,

Each day,

Revealed his dire state,

Desperate,

To find himself,

A beloved son,

In his father's eyes.

With nothing,

He had to find something,

To cling to,

In that foreign land.

After many dreaded days,

He met a humble merchant,

Tending and selling pigs,

Who would give him a place to stay.

Though unclean,

He was taught all his life,

Now those pigs in the pen,

Were the only answer,

To his dilemma.

Among the unclean,

He felt his spirit,

Broken and contrite,

And lifted his head,

A clear blue sky,

The same sky,

Above the green field,

Where he grew up,

The memory forgotten,

Now yearning.

The Younger Son

Just another day,

In the City,

As with any other day,

But so much has changed.

Things could not be undone,

Time moves,

But only forward.

Oh, this hunger so deep,

To the point,

Of tasting death,

To the point,

Of wanting to eat the pods,

Of the unclean.

Was it a mistake?

Following my heart,

Embarking on the fateful journey,

To the City,

The City that had left me.

I finally learned,

Wisdom found in pain and suffering,

That a human heart,

Deceitful above all things,

Especially blinding,

The heart of a youth,

Passionate beyond measure,

Dreaming of conquering the world,

Only to be brought down,

By the hands of reality,

The world is,

Utterly unforgiving.

The Teacher

Repentance is,

A change of mind,

That only comes,

When sorrow so deep,

That grieves the very depth of a soul.

The bottom of the bottoms,

That one must reach,

To see clearer than clearest,

Of where one is,

Not physically,

But spiritually.

And there he was,

The younger son,

Spent thoroughly in cries and tears,

Could taste the death itself,

Yet alive.

That ember within,

Almost dying,

Came alive instead.

He did not know how or why,

But the dying ember,

Would ignite.

The yearning so faint,

Yet so real,

A voice unavoidable,

Homeward bound,

It whispered,

Then it proclaimed.

Homeward bound,

He must.

The Younger Son

Where did it all start?

When my contentment started to ebb away,

When the grass was greener,

On the other side,

When my father's hand on my shoulder,

Felt heavier,

When my brother was no longer a brother,

But a firstborn,

When the Heavenly One,

Was no longer the One.

Now with my feet in the mud of the pigpen,

I understand,

My place is,

My father's,

My place always has been,

My father's.

Homeward bound,

That I would,

Only if I could,

But my disgrace,

Too heavy to lift,

My defiance,

Too loud to silence,

Going back,

Impossible as time itself.

Could I try?

Futile,

A dark voice says.

Shall I try?

You must,

Another voice says,

A gentle whisper,

Tender and loving.

Summoning the strength within,

However feeble it may be,

I choose to see,

How even my father's servants,

Have plenty to eat,

While my mouth can find nothing to eat,

Yes, I will go back to my father and say:

My father,

I have sinned against heaven,

And against you,

I am no longer worthy to be called,

Your son,

Only make me like one of your servants,

I would be content,

I would be grateful,

To be within your care.

With these words of repentance,

Homeward bound,

I will,

Leaving behind,

The City,

The mirage,

With everything in it.

Now I see,

All my tears had watered my soul,

To grow within,

All my cries had taught my mind,

To see within,

None has been wasted,

In the shadow of,

Sorrow upon sorrow.

My farewell to this City,

Not bittersweet but only sweet,

Forgiving all the souls,

Who could only see,

My money,

And not my being.

Now I will be on my way,

Back to where it all began,

That baby's first cry,

My origin,

Home.

The Father

Days turned to weeks,

Weeks turned to months,

Yet no sign of my dear son.

But today,

A glimmer of hope,

A neighbor who traveled,

Through a distant village,

Said he thought he saw my dear son,

Not for sure,

But perhaps so,

He looked much different,

He said.

Hence I look,

To the distant horizon,

Hoping to see,

The answer to my prayer,

Cried out day and night.

Even a tiny silhouette of a figure,

Above the distant horizon,

I would recognize,

My heart will see,

Even before my eyes.

Wherever he may be,

May the Heavenly One,

Hasten his steps,

Lift up his soul,

Level his path,

Godspeed my son,

But this time,

Homeward bound.

The Younger Son

The path home,

I know well,

Yet I do not know,

What awaits me there,

Fear of rejection,

Relief of rest,

Intertwined within my heart,

I continue on.

With every breath,

With every step,

Closer I am,

To my journey's end,

I now realize,

My journey was,

Meant to be a full circle,

After all,

Ending where it all began,

My father's farewell,

In which I now see,

His grace,

Mercy,

Patience,

Surrender.

Press on my soul,

The circle is almost complete,

A new life awaits,

Even as a servant,

Which is still far better,

Than who I was in the City,

No more looking back,

My sight set only ahead,

Press on.

The Father

Oh, what a gracious sight,

I see him,

My dear son.

A tiny silhouette of a figure in the distance,

All others may not see,

But my eyes those of a father,

See his son.

A second is too long,

For me to wait,

Let me run to you.

Run, run,

With all my being,

To receive the son,

I thought I had lost.

Oh, I dreamed of this every night,

Only to awake in the brutal reality,

Of the absence of you.

But now the reality is,

The sweetest witnessing of your return.

Press on,

My feet,

My arms,

My whole body.

My worries and sorrow are lifted,

New hope abound,

Both of my sons in my arms,

My life is full again.

I can see him clearer now,

Glory and honor to the Heavenly One,

Who graciously granted,

This old man's prayer.

My dear son,

You are home.

The Teacher

The circle is indeed complete,

The return,

The reunion,

Under the same blue sky,

That the younger son looked up,

In that foreign land.

The younger son tried to utter:

My father,

I have sinned against heaven,

And against you,

I am no longer worthy to be called,

Your son,

But the father's embrace,

So dear,

Melted his words into,

Only tears,

Of repentance.

The father urged his servants:

Quickly bring out the best robe,

Put it on him,

Put a ring on his hand,

Sandals on his feet,

Prepare the fattened calf,

Let us eat and celebrate,

For my son was dead,

And has come to life again,

He was lost,

And has been found.

The younger son was indeed dead,

Dead to his old self,

Young and restless,

Lost in the mirage of the City,

But now he was alive,

A renewed mind,

That could see,

What his father could see,

A life in the field,

His destiny carefully handcrafted,

By no other than the Heavenly One,

Learning the truth,

Working the field was his part,

While the harvest was not,

As such,

Working on his character was his part,

But whom he would eventually become was
not,

Only that of the realm,

Of the Heavenly One.

Finally he learned,

Obedience and surrender,

The very purpose of his being,

Wonderfully made,

By the divine hands of the Heavenly One,

Who was once again the One,

In his heart.

In the distance,

The older son was returning,

Another hard day in the field,

Why the sound of music and dancing,

He wondered and asked,

The answer of a servant,

His heart did not want to hear:

Your brother has returned,

And your father has killed the fattened calf

to celebrate,

For he has received him back,

Safe and sound.

The anger within,

He could not contain,

No, I will not enter the house,

To celebrate,

For there is nothing,

To celebrate.

Hearing his older son,

The father knew,

His place was once again,

The seat of humility,

Pleading.

The Older Son

My father,

My father,

Why do you treat me this way?

Do you only see your younger son?

All these years as your firstborn,

No command of yours,

Went unfollowed,

My obedience,

My banner,

Your words,

Heeded with no hesitance,

Laboring and toiling,

Accepted as my destiny.

Yet even a young goat,

You did not spare,

Ever,

For me to celebrate with my friends,

But when this son of yours came back,

Who has devoured your wealth,

With prostitutes,

You killed the fattened calf,

To celebrate,

Like never before.

Did he not betray our family?

Did he not exploit your patience?

Did he not treat you as if you were dead?

Where is the punishment,

Befitting his sins?

How is this fair?

Injustice,

Partiality,

Favoritism,

My very soul,

Is crushed and defeated,

By your grace and mercy,

Without reasoning,

For this prodigal son.

The Father

My dear son,

My firstborn,

The pride of the family,

You have been always with me,

All that is mine,

Is yours,

Your birthright,

Is yours,

Your future,

Is yours.

But we had to celebrate and rejoice,

For this brother of yours,

Was dead,

And is alive,

Was lost,

And is found.

The Teacher

Hence the story ends,

The response of the older son,

We would never know.

Why the story?

What is the teaching?

Perfect,

Is our Heavenly Father.

Prodigal,

That we all are,

Every,

Single,

One of us.

Love, grace and mercy,

So undeserved,

Every,

Single,

One of us.

Our obedience,

Not a merit,

But a response,

As we should,

As His children.

Those in His bosom,

We labor and toil,

Knowing fully well,

All that is His,

Is ours in the end.

Those who are wandering,

We seek,

What life is all about,

Why so much suffering,

With so little happiness.

Come,

He beckons,

When you hear that voice,

A faint whisper,

Or a loud cry,

Do not quell it,

But let it sink in,

Let it lead you,

Homeward bound,

However far it may be,

However long it may take,

Press on,

Press on,

Home.

Welcome to the New

ILLUMINATION
PUBLISHERS
www.ipibooks.com

SPEAKING OF GOD — DR. JOHN M. OAKES

Spiritual Transformation — Cresenda Jones

MESSIANIC JUDAISM — DOUGLAS JACOBY

Go in the Strength You Have — Rayola Osanya

A HOUSE OF PRAYER — C. SCOTT DAVIS

LOVE, LAUGHTER, AND LAW — RON AND LINDA BRUMLEY

Jesus and Mental Health — Marvin K. Lucas

WHAT NOW, GOD? — JEANIE SHAW

SINGLES MINISTRY CAN CHANGE THE WORLD — FERNANDO ALEJANDRO

Mindpowered Singles — CRESENDA JONES

Journey of the SOUL — Timothy Sumerlin, Editor

THE UPWARD CALL — PAT GEMPEL, EDITOR

CALLING OUT THE PEOPLE OF GOD — DOUGLAS JACOBY

PAIN KILLER — R.K. McKEAN

The Sacred Journey — Jeanie Shaw and Friends

WILDFIRE — DAREN OVERSTREET

The Recovery Journey — TIMOTHY SUMERLIN, Ph.D.

This Doesn't Feel Like Love Either — LAMBS